101 Positive Affirmations for Women

TRANSFORM YOUR LIFE WITH DAILY PRACTICES FOR
CONFIDENCE, EMPOWERMENT, AND LASTING JOY

MELISSA G WILSON

Copyright © 2024 by Melissa G Wilson

All rights reserved.

No part of this book may be reproduced in any form or by any electronic or mechanical means, including information storage and retrieval systems, without written permission from the author, except for the use of brief quotations in a book review.

For my Family

Thank you for all your love and support that has helped make me who I am.

Contents

Preface vii

1. Confidence Affirmations 1
2. Empowerment Affirmations 15
3. Lasting Joy Affirmations 29
   Bonus #1 43
   Cultivating Peaceful and Restful Sleep
   Bonus #2 51
   Extreme Self Care

   About the Author 75
   Before You Go 79

Preface

Dear Reader,

Hello; I'm Melissa G. Wilson. I'm so grateful to be able to share my latest book, "101 Positive Affirmations for Women: Transform Your Life with Daily Practices for Confidence, Empowerment, and Lasting Joy," with you. This book represents the culmination of my life's work and passion, which, for two decades, has been dedicated to empowering women through my writing, speaking, and coaching.

My leadership and motivational literature journey has been challenging while also incredibly rewarding. With five best-selling books to my name, I've had the privilege of touching the lives of thousands of women worldwide. Each book I've written has been fueled by a singular mission: to help readers recognize their innate strength, embrace their potential, and live lives of purpose and joy.

This book is more than just another book to me. It's a powerful tool born from years of research, personal experiences, and countless interactions with women from all walks of life. I've seen firsthand the transformative power of positive self-talk and intentional action. With this book, I wanted to create a resource that makes this powerful combination accessible to every woman daily.

My background in training, coaching, and mentoring women has helped me to approach affirmations uniquely. By pairing each affirmation with a specific daily practice, I've aimed to bridge the gap between thought and action, helping you think positively and embody that positivity in your daily life.

The structure of this book—focusing on confidence, empowerment, and lasting joy—reflects the cornerstones of a fulfilling life for women. These are the areas where I've seen women struggle the most but also where I've witnessed the most profound transformations. The subtitle, "Transform Your Life with Daily Practices," encapsulates my belief in the power of consistent, intentional action to create lasting change.

I created this book to be more than a collection of affirmations. It's a daily companion in your journey of self-discovery and growth. It's a tool to help you start and end each day with intention and positivity. It's a reminder of your worth, power, and capacity for joy.

I hope "101 Positive Affirmations for Women" will catalyze positive change in your life. It will help you silence your inner critic, step into your power, and cultivate a deep, lasting sense of joy. Remember, you have within you everything you need to create the life you desire. These affirmations and daily practices are here to help you unlock that potential.

I designed this book to take you through a transformative journey of self-discovery and personal growth. The structure I chose was carefully crafted to address three fundamental aspects of your life as a woman.

To this end, each section contains 33-34 affirmations, creating a balanced and comprehensive approach to personal development.

CONFIDENCE - IT'S ABOUT TRUST

Did you know that the word "confidence" comes from the Latin root "fidere," meaning "to trust"? This section is your gateway to building trust in yourself, the cornerstone of your personal growth and success.

The Confidence section lays the bedrock for your transformative journey with 34 carefully crafted affirmations.

As you dive into these affirmations, you will:

PREFACE

- Boost your self-esteem to new heights
- Silence that pesky inner critic once and for all
- Discover the true depth of your self-worth

Each affirmation is a powerful tool designed to help you trust in your abilities, judgments, and inherent value. As you practice these affirmations daily, you'll feel your self-trust grow stronger, creating a solid foundation for empowerment and joy in the following sections.

Remember, confidence isn't about being perfect—it's about trusting yourself to handle whatever comes your way.

EMPOWERMENT: UNLOCKING YOUR INNER STRENGTH

In the Empowerment section, you will discover 34 affirmations designed to help you tap into your innate power and take charge of your life. Building on the foundation of confidence, this section invites you to explore and embrace your capabilities.

These crafted affirmations will:

- Awaken your personal power
- Inspire you to take action
- Remind you of your incredible abilities

PREFACE

There are 34 affirmations here, just like in the Confidence section. This balance reflects the deep connection between confidence and empowerment. As one grows, so does the other.

As you work through these empowerment affirmations, allow yourself to recognize and celebrate your strengths. Remember, empowerment isn't about dominating others. It's about standing firmly in your own power and using it to create positive change in your life and the world around you.

Take your time with each affirmation. Let its message resonate with you. You may find that some affirmations speak to you more strongly than others. That's perfectly natural. Use what serves you best on your journey to empowerment.

LASTING JOY: NURTURING YOUR INNER HAPPINESS

The final section of our journey is focused on Lasting Joy. Here, you'll find 33 affirmations designed to help you cultivate a more enduring sense of happiness and contentment.

Building on the confidence and empowerment you've developed, these affirmations gently encourage you to:

- Appreciate the present moment
- Maintain a balanced outlook

- Find contentment within yourself

While I can't promise perpetual bliss, these affirmations can help you develop resilience and a more positive perspective, even during challenging times. They serve as gentle reminders to look for joy in your daily life and to nurture your inner well-being.

Remember, lasting joy isn't about being happy all the time. It's about finding moments of peace, gratitude, and satisfaction throughout your day. These affirmations are tools to help you recognize and cultivate those moments.

As you work through these affirmations, be patient with yourself. Building lasting joy is a gradual process unique to each individual. Some days may feel easier than others, and that's okay. The goal is progress, not perfection.

AMPLIFYING AFFIRMATIONS

A unique feature of this book is the inclusion of application suggestions. They follow each affirmation. I designed these suggestions to amplify the impact of each affirmation beyond the traditional practice times. While reciting these affirmations when you first rise and before you fall asleep (a practice known as "book-ending") is recommended, the additional suggestions provide ways to embody and internalize the affirmations throughout your day.

For example, an affirmation about confidence might be

followed by a suggestion to stand in a power pose while reciting it. An empowerment affirmation might be paired with a visualization exercise. A joy-focused affirmation could be accompanied by a prompt to engage in a related positive action.

These amplification techniques serve several purposes:

1. They help deepen the affirmations' impact by engaging multiple senses and modes of learning.
2. They provide practical ways to integrate affirmations into daily life, making them more than words, but lived experiences.
3. They offer variety in practice, which can help maintain interest and commitment to the affirmation routine.
4. They bridge the gap between morning and evening practices, allowing the power of the affirmations to resonate throughout the day.

By "book-ending" your day with these affirmations and their amplification techniques, you create a robust framework for personal growth. This practice helps to set a positive tone for the day ahead and allows for reflection and reinforcement of positive thoughts before sleep. Over time, this consistent practice can lead to significant shifts in mindset, behavior, and overall well-being.

CHAPTER 1
Confidence Affirmations

The word "confidence" has a fascinating etymological history. Let's explore its origins and evolution and then look at some empowering quotes about confidence for women.

ETYMOLOGY OF "CONFIDENCE"

The word "confidence" comes from the Latin word "confidentia," which means "firmly trusting, bold." It's derived from the Latin "confidere," meaning "to have full trust or reliance," which is formed from:

1. "com-" (meaning "with")
2. "fidere" (meaning "to trust")

The word entered the English language in the mid-14th century, initially meaning "reliance on one's ability or qualities." Over time, its usage expanded to include a sense of self-assurance and certainty.

EVOLUTION OF THE CONCEPT

The concept of confidence has evolved significantly over time. In earlier societies, confidence was often associated with social status, wealth, or physical strength. As societies progressed, the understanding of confidence expanded to include mental and emotional aspects. In the 20th and 21st centuries, with the rise of psychology and self-help literature, confidence has become recognized as a crucial element of personal development and success.

Now, let's look at some quotes that emphasize confidence for women, along with context about the speakers:

> "I was always looking outside myself for strength and confidence, but it comes from within. It is there all the time."
>
> ANNA FREUD

Anna Freud, daughter of Sigmund Freud, was a pioneering psychoanalyst who founded child psychoanalysis. Her work in psychology required immense confidence, as she was operating in a male-dominated field. This quote reflects her understanding that true confidence is an internal quality, not dependent on external validation. This self-reliant mindset undoubtedly bolstered her success in establishing new theories in child psychology.

> "Think like a queen. A queen is not afraid to fail. Failure is another stepping stone to greatness."
>
> OPRAH WINFREY

Oprah Winfrey, media executive, actress, and philanthropist, built a media empire from humble beginnings. Her journey from poverty to becoming one of the most influential women in the world required tremendous confidence. This quote emphasizes the importance of resilience and viewing failures as opportunities for growth. Oprah's success in various ventures, from her talk show to her network OWN, demonstrates how this confident approach to challenges has propelled her career.

> "I do not try to dance better than anyone else. I only try to dance better than myself."
>
> MIKHAIL BARYSHNIKOV

While Mikhail Baryshnikov is male, this quote is particularly relevant to women in competitive fields. Baryshnikov, one of the greatest ballet dancers of the 20th century, emphasizes the importance of self-improvement rather than comparison to others. This mindset is crucial for building genuine confidence. Women in various fields, from arts to sciences, can apply this philosophy to focus on personal growth and excellence, rather than being discouraged by comparisons to others.

These quotes emphasize different aspects of confidence: internal strength, resilience in the face of failure, and focus on personal growth. Each speaker's success in their respective fields illustrates how these confident mindsets contributed to their achievements, providing inspiring examples for women across various domains.

Confidence is the foundation for personal growth and success. These affirmations are offered to help you boost your self-esteem, silence your inner critic, and help you recognize your inherent worth.

Incorporating confidence-building statements into your daily routine will nurture a strong sense of self-assurance that will empower you in all areas of life. As you practice, you may find yourself:

- Trusting your judgment more readily
- Embracing your unique qualities and strengths
- Speaking up for yourself with assurance
- Pursuing opportunities with less hesitation
- Bouncing back from setbacks more easily
- Radiating self-assurance in your interactions with others

Remember, confidence isn't about being perfect or fearless. It's about trusting in your ability to handle whatever comes your way. These affirmations will help you cultivate that trust, allowing you to step out of your comfort zone, take calculated risks, and reach for your goals.

By consistently practicing these affirmations, you're training your mind to focus on your strengths and capabilities rather than your doubts and fears. Over time, you may notice a shift in how you perceive yourself and interact with the world around you.

Embrace these affirmations as a daily practice. Watch as your confidence grows, opening doors to new opportunities and experiences. As your self-assurance strengthens, you may find it positively impacting every aspect of your life, from your relationships to your career and personal achievements.

THE AFFIRMATIONS FOR CONFIDENCE

1. I am confident in my abilities and trust my judgment.

> Stand tall with your shoulders back as you say this, physically embodying confidence. This posture helps activate your body's innate confidence, reinforcing your self-trust.

2. I embrace my unique beauty and radiate self-love.

> Look in the mirror and smile at yourself while repeating this affirmation. This practice helps you develop a positive self-image and counteracts negative self-talk.

3. My voice deserves to be heard, and my opinions matter.

> Practice saying this before entering meetings or discussions to boost your confidence in speaking up. This preparation primes you to contribute valuable insights and assert your presence.

4. I am worthy of respect and command it through my actions.

> Stand in a power pose (hands on hips, feet apart) while saying this affirmation. This stance increases testosterone and decreases cortisol, hormones associated with confidence and stress.

5. I trust my intuition and make decisions with confidence.

> Place your hand on your gut as you say this, connecting with your intuitive center. This physical gesture reinforces the mind-body connection and helps you tune into your inner wisdom.

6. I am capable of achieving anything I set my mind to.

> Visualize yourself accomplishing a goal as you repeat this affirmation. This mental rehearsal prepares your mind for success and boosts your belief in your capabilities.

7. I embrace challenges as opportunities to showcase my strengths.

> Say this before tackling a difficult task, reframing challenges as positive experiences. This mindset shift helps you approach obstacles with enthusiasm rather than fear.

8. I am comfortable in my skin and love my body unconditionally.

> Touch different parts of your body with gratitude as you say this affirmation. This practice fosters body positivity and appreciation for your physical self.

9. I radiate confidence and inspire others with my presence.

> Practice saying this while making eye contact with yourself in the mirror. This exercise helps you project confidence outwardly and recognize your own inspiring qualities.

10. I deserve success and can claim it confidently.

> As you repeat this, visualize yourself accepting an award or achieving a goal. This visualization technique reinforces your belief in your worthiness of success.

11. I trust in my ability to handle any situation with grace.

> Take a deep breath and center yourself before saying this affirmation. This calming technique helps you access your inner resources and composure.

12. I am proud of my accomplishments and celebrate my successes.

> List three recent achievements, then say this affirmation while reviewing them. This practice cultivates gratitude and reinforces your sense of accomplishment.

13. I embrace my femininity as a source of power and strength.

> As you say this, place your hand on your heart, connecting with your feminine energy. This gesture helps you tap into your innate feminine power and wisdom.

14. I am confident in expressing my needs and desires.

> Practice saying this before having meaningful conversations about your needs. This preparation empowers you to communicate assertively and clearly.

15. I trust in my path and journey, comparing myself to no one.

> Say this while walking, focusing on your unique journey forward. This physical movement reinforces the idea of progressing on your path.

16. I am worthy of love and respect, starting with self-love.

> Hug yourself while saying this affirmation, physically embodying self-love. This self-nurturing gesture helps cultivate a deep sense of self-worth.

17. I embrace my imperfections as part of my unique beauty.

> Look in the mirror and appreciate your unique features as you say this. This practice helps you reframe perceived flaws as aspects of your beauty.

18. I am confident in my ability to learn and grow daily.

> Say this before starting a new task or learning experience. This mindset primes you for growth and helps you approach new challenges enthusiastically.

19. I trust in my capacity to overcome any obstacle.

> Visualize yourself climbing over a barrier as you repeat this affirmation. This mental imagery reinforces your belief in your ability to overcome challenges.

20. I radiate inner and outer beauty.

> Smile warmly while saying this, allowing your inner beauty to shine through. This practice helps align your inner feelings with your outer expression.

21. I am confident in setting and maintaining healthy boundaries.

> Practice saying this before entering social situations or relationships. This preparation empowers you to assert your needs and limits confidently.

22. I trust in my ability to make wise decisions for my life.

> Close your eyes and take a deep breath before saying this, centering yourself. This moment of mindfulness helps you connect with your inner wisdom.

23. I embrace my body as a powerful vessel of strength and vitality.

> Say this while doing a gentle stretch or yoga pose, connecting with your body. This physical practice reinforces your appreciation for your body's capabilities.

25. I confidently pursue my passions and dreams.

> Write down a dream or goal, then affirm while holding the paper. This tangible representation of your aspirations reinforces your commitment to pursuing them.

26. I trust my ability to handle criticism constructively without blaming myself.

> After receiving feedback, repeat this while writing how to use it for growth. This practice helps reframe criticism as a tool for improvement rather than a personal attack.

27. I radiate self-assurance in all aspects of my life.

> Walk confidently while saying this, embodying self-assurance in your movement. This physical practice helps align your body language with your inner confidence.

28. I am confident in balancing multiple roles with grace.

> Visualize yourself successfully juggling different aspects of your life as you say this. This mental imagery reinforces your belief in your ability to manage various responsibilities.

29. I trust in my unique perspective and value my insights.

> Before sharing your thoughts, repeat this to boost confidence in your viewpoint. This affirmation empowers you to contribute your unique ideas and perspectives.

30. I embrace my intelligence and mental capabilities.

> Tap your forehead gently while saying this, acknowledging your mental strengths. This gesture reinforces your connection with your intellectual abilities.

31. I am confident in my ability to create positive change.

> Say this before acting on a goal, reinforcing your power to effect change. This practice primes you for taking meaningful action towards your objectives.

32. I trust in my resilience to bounce back from any setback.

> Visualize yourself as a rubber band, stretching and snapping back as you repeat this. This imagery reinforces your belief in your ability to recover from challenges.

33. I radiate confidence in my unique style and self-expression.

> Say this while getting dressed, appreciating your personal style. This practice helps you embrace and celebrate your individuality.

34. I am worthy of respect and admiration, including from myself.

> Look in the mirror and give yourself a respectful nod as you say this affirmation. This gesture of self-respect reinforces your inherent worthiness.

CHAPTER 2
Empowerment Affirmations

The word "empowerment" is derived from the base word "power," which comes from the Latin "potere," meaning "to be able."

1. The prefix "em-" is a variant of "en-," meaning "put into" or "cover with."
2. The suffix "-ment" denotes the result of an action or a state of being.

"Empower" as a verb first appeared in the 17th century, meaning "to invest with authority, authorize." However, the noun "empowerment" in its modern usage didn't emerge until the mid-20th century.

The concept gained prominence in the 1960s and 1970s, aligning with civil rights movements and feminism. By the 1980s and 1990s, it had become widely used in management theory, social work, education, and international development.

Now, let's look at some quotes that emphasize empowerment for women:

> "We need to accept that we won't always make the right decisions, that we'll screw up royally sometimes – understanding that failure is not the opposite of success, it's part of success."
>
> ARIANNA HUFFINGTON

Arianna Huffington, co-founder of The Huffington Post and founder of Thrive Global, has pioneered digital media and wellness. This quote emphasizes the importance of resilience and learning from failures, key aspects of empowerment. Huffington's journey from immigrant to leading a major media company illustrates how embracing failure as part of the growth process has contributed to her success. Her work promoting work-life balance and well-being further demonstrates how this empowering mindset has influenced her business and personal development approach.

"The most difficult thing is the decision to act. The rest is merely tenacity. The fears are paper tigers. You can do anything you decide to do."

AMELIA EARHART

Amelia Earhart, the first female aviator to fly solo across the Atlantic Ocean, embodies courage and determination. This quote highlights the power of decision-making and perseverance in fear. Earhart's groundbreaking achievements in aviation during a time dominated by men showcase how this empowered mindset drove her to break barriers and inspire generations of women to pursue their dreams, regardless of societal expectations.

"I've learned that people will forget what you said, people will forget what you did, but people will never forget how you made them feel."

MAYA ANGELOU

Maya Angelou, renowned poet, memoirist, and civil rights activist, used her voice to empower others through her writing and speeches. This quote emphasizes the lasting impact of empathy and human connection. Angelou's remarkable career as a writer and her influence as a voice for social justice demonstrate how this focus on human dignity and emotional impact can create profound change.

Her ability to inspire and empower others through her words and actions has left an indelible mark on literature and civil rights.

These quotes highlight different facets of empowerment: embracing failure as part of success, overcoming fear through action, and recognizing the power of human connection. Each speaker's success in their respective fields — media and wellness, aviation, and literature and activism — illustrates how these empowering mindsets have contributed to their achievements and their ability to inspire and uplift others.

> "We do not need magic to transform our world. We carry all the power we need inside ourselves already."
>
> J.K. ROWLING

J.K. Rowling, author of the Harry Potter series, went from being a single mother living on welfare to becoming one of the world's best-selling authors. This quote emphasizes the innate power within individuals to create change. Rowling's journey from adversity to literary and philanthropic success exemplifies how recognizing and harnessing one's inner strength can lead to transformative outcomes.

These quotes highlight different aspects of empowerment: giving voice to the voiceless, recognizing inherent power, and believing in one's ability to create change. Each speaker's success in their respective fields — activism, literature, and philanthropy — demonstrates how these empowering mindsets have contributed to their achievements and ability to impact the world positively.

Empowerment is also about recognizing and harnessing your inner strength to create your desired life. These affirmations are crafted to awaken your power, encourage you to take charge of your life, and remind you of your inherent capabilities.

Incorporating these empowering statements into your daily routine will cultivate a mindset of possibility and action. As you practice, you may find yourself more confidently pursuing your goals, standing up for your beliefs, and creating positive change in your life and the world around you.

These affirmations will help you:

- Recognize and embrace your power
- Challenge limiting beliefs and societal expectations
- Develop confidence in your abilities and decisions
- Advocate for yourself and others
- Create positive change in your life and community
- Pursue your dreams and ambitions with determination
- Build resilience in the face of adversity

Remember, true empowerment comes from within. These affirmations are tools to help you tap into the strength and wisdom you already possess. As you practice, you may become more assertive, resilient, and proactive in shaping your life and impacting your world.

Embrace these affirmations as a daily practice. Watch as you grow into a more empowered version of yourself, capable of achieving your goals and living life on your terms.

THE EMPOWERMENT AFFIRMATIONS

35. I am the architect of my own life and destiny.

> Say this while visualizing yourself building your ideal life, brick by brick. This visualization reinforces your sense of control over your life's direction and empowers you to make conscious choices.

36. I can create positive change in my life and the world.

> Before taking action on a goal, repeat this to reinforce your ability to make a difference. This practice primes you for meaningful action and reminds you of your potential impact.

37. I embrace my strength and resilience as a woman.

> Stand in a power pose while saying this, physically embodying your strength. This posture activates feelings of confidence and power, reinforcing your belief in your capabilities.

38. I am empowered to pursue my dreams unapologetically.

> Write down a big goal, then say this affirmation while holding the paper to your heart. This physical act connects your aspirations with your emotional center, strengthening your commitment.

39. I trust in my ability to overcome any obstacle.

> Visualize yourself climbing over a mountain as you repeat this affirmation. This mental imagery reinforces your belief in your ability to overcome challenges, no matter how daunting.

40. I am capable of achieving greatness on my own terms.

> Close your eyes and envision your personal definition of greatness while saying this. This practice helps you align your actions with your unique vision of success.

41. I embrace my power to say no and set healthy boundaries.

> Practice saying this before entering situations where you need to assert boundaries. This preparation empowers you to maintain your personal limits and respect your own needs.

42. I am deserving of success and actively create opportunities for myself.

> Visualize doors of opportunity opening as you repeat this affirmation. This imagery reinforces your belief in your worthiness and ability to create your own success.

43. I trust in my ability to lead and inspire others.

> Say this before taking on a leadership role or task, boosting your leadership confidence. This affirmation helps you step into leadership roles with assurance and purpose.

44. I am empowered to make choices that align with my values and goals.

> Write down your core values, then affirm them while reviewing them. This practice reinforces your commitment to living authentically and making decisions that reflect your true self.

45. I embrace my feminine power as a source of strength and wisdom.

> Place your hand on your heart, connecting with your feminine energy as you say this. This gesture helps you tap into and appreciate your innate feminine wisdom and power.

46. I can balance all aspects of my life with grace and ease.

> Visualize yourself successfully juggling different life aspects as you repeat this. This mental practice reinforces your ability to maintain harmony in various areas of your life.

47. I trust my ability to rise above societal expectations and limitations.

> Say this while imagining yourself breaking through a glass ceiling. This visualization empowers you to challenge and overcome societal constraints.

48. I am empowered to use my voice for positive change.

> Practice saying this before speaking up in meetings or public forums. This preparation boosts your confidence in expressing your ideas and advocating for positive change.

49. I embrace my right to take up space and be heard.

> Stand with your feet firmly planted and arms outstretched as you say this. This physical stance reinforces your right to be present and acknowledged.

50. I am deserving of equal opportunities and fair treatment.

> Say this before entering negotiations or discussions about your rights. This affirmation reminds you of your worth and empowers you to advocate for fairness.

51. I trust my capacity to learn, grow, and adapt to any situation.

> Before starting a new task or learning experience, repeat this affirmation. This practice opens your mind to new possibilities and reinforces your adaptability.

52. I am empowered to break free from limiting beliefs and stereotypes.

> Visualize yourself breaking chains as you say this, symbolizing freedom from limitations. This imagery reinforces your ability to overcome internal and external constraints.

53. I embrace my ability to create and innovate in my field.

> Say this before starting a creative project or brainstorming session. This affirmation primes your mind for innovative thinking and boosts your creative confidence.

54. I am capable of achieving financial independence and abundance.

> Repeat this while creating a financial plan or budget, reinforcing your financial empowerment. This practice aligns your mindset with your financial goals and actions.

55. I trust intuition to guide me towards my highest good.

> As you say this, place your hand on your stomach (your "gut"), connecting with your intuition. This physical gesture reinforces your connection to your inner wisdom.

56. I am empowered to prioritize my well-being and self-care.

> Say this while engaging in a self-care activity, reinforcing its importance. This practice validates your right to care for yourself and prioritize your well-being.

57. I embrace my right to pursue happiness and fulfillment.

> Smile genuinely while saying this, connecting the affirmation with happiness. This physical expression reinforces the positive emotions associated with pursuing your happiness.

58. I deserve respect in all my personal and professional relationships.

> Practice saying this before entering meaningful relationships or collaborations. This affirmation sets a standard for how you expect to be treated in all your interactions.

59. I trust in my ability to make a positive impact in my community.

> Before engaging in volunteer work or community service, repeat this affirmation. This practice reinforces your belief in your ability to contribute meaningfully to your community.

60. I am empowered to challenge and change unfair systems.

> Visualize yourself as an agent of change as you say this affirmation. This imagery reinforces your power to create positive systemic change.

61. I embrace and use my unique talents to their fullest potential.

> List your top three strengths, then say this affirmation while focusing on each one. This practice helps you recognize and appreciate your unique abilities.

62. I am capable of creating healthy, fulfilling relationships.

> Say this before meeting new people or nurturing existing relationships. This affirmation sets a positive intention for your interactions and relationships.

63. I trust in my resilience to overcome adversity and emerge stronger.

> Repeat this while reflecting on your strength and growth after facing a challenge. This practice reinforces your belief in your ability to bounce back from difficulties.

64. I am empowered to define success on my own terms.

> Write your definition of success, then affirm while reading it. This exercise helps you align your actions with your personal vision of success.

65. I embrace my power to forgive and let go of past hurts.

> Visualize releasing a balloon while saying this, symbolizing letting go of past pain. This imagery reinforces your ability to release negativity and move forward.

66. I deserve love, respect, and kindness from others.

> Look in the mirror and give yourself a warm, loving smile as you say this. This self-love practice reinforces your worthiness of positive treatment from others.

67. I trust in my ability to create positive change in my career.

> Repeat this to boost your professional confidence before a job interview or career move. This affirmation empowers you to take bold steps in your professional life.

68. I am empowered to advocate for myself and others.

> Practice saying this before standing up for yourself or others in challenging situations. This preparation strengthens your resolve to speak up for what's right.

CHAPTER 3
Lasting Joy Affirmations

The word "joy" has an interesting etymology and evolution. Let's explore its origins and then look at some empowering quotes related to joy and confidence for women.

ETYMOLOGY AND EVOLUTION OF "JOY"

The word "joy" comes from the Old French "joie," which in turn comes from the Latin "gaudia," the plural of "gaudium" meaning "joy, delight."

1. The Latin "gaudium" is derived from the verb "gaudere," meaning "to rejoice."
2. The Indo-European root is "*gau-," which is related to rejoicing and being glad.

"Joy" entered English in the 12th century, initially meaning "a feeling of great pleasure and happiness." Over time, its usage has expanded to encompass a range of positive emotions, from contentment to elation.

The concept of joy has evolved in psychological and philosophical discourse. In recent years, there has been increased focus on joy as a component of well-being and mental health, distinct from mere pleasure or happiness.

Now, let's look at some quotes that emphasize joy and confidence for women, along with context about the speakers:

> "Find out what gives you joy and do it. Because that is your gift to the world."
>
> DOLLY PARTON

Dolly Parton, renowned country music singer-songwriter, actress, and businesswoman, has built an empire based on her talents and personality. This quote reflects her belief in the power of pursuing one's passions. Parton's success across multiple industries demonstrates how following her joy in music and performance has led to personal fulfillment, allowing her to impact others positively. Her confidence in her unique style and abilities has been a critical factor in her enduring career and philanthropic efforts.

"The most effective way to do it, is to do it."

AMELIA EARHART

While this quote doesn't explicitly mention joy, it embodies the confidence and action-oriented approach that often leads to joy. Amelia Earhart, the first female aviator to fly solo across the Atlantic Ocean, lived by these words. Her confidence in taking action led her to achieve numerous aviation records and brought her joy in pushing boundaries. Earhart's approach to life and her achievements inspire women to pursue their passions confidently, even in male-dominated fields.

"If you're not having fun, you're doing something wrong."

GROUCHO MARX

Although Groucho Marx was not a woman, this quote is particularly relevant to women seeking balance and fulfillment in their lives. It emphasizes the importance of finding joy in one's pursuits. We can look at how successful women have applied this principle.

For example, Shonda Rhimes, creator of hit TV shows like "Grey's Anatomy" and "Scandal," has spoken about rediscovering her joy in work and life. In her book "Year of Yes," she describes how saying yes to things that scared her led to more joy and success in both her personal and professional life. This approach aligns with Marx's quote, as Rhimes found that she needed to change her approach when she wasn't enjoying her work.

These quotes emphasize different aspects of joy and confidence: pursuing what brings you joy, taking confident action, and making sure you enjoy what you do. The success of figures like Dolly Parton, Amelia Earhart, and Shonda Rhimes in their respective fields illustrates how these joy-centric and confident mindsets have contributed to their achievements and personal fulfillment.

Joy is not just a fleeting emotion, but a sustainable state of being that you can cultivate and maintain. These affirmations help you tap into your innate capacity for joy, appreciate life's simple pleasures, and maintain a positive outlook even in challenging times.

By incorporating these joy-focused affirmations into your daily routine, you'll train your mind to seek out and create happiness in your everyday experiences. You'll develop a greater sense of gratitude, resilience, and contentment. As you practice, you may find yourself more readily noticing the good in your life, finding silver linings under challenging situations, and experiencing a more profound sense of fulfillment.

Remember, joy depends not on external circumstances but on your internal perspective. These affirmations will help you cultivate that joyful perspective, allowing you to experience more happiness, peace, and satisfaction in all areas of your life. As you embrace joy as a practice, you may find that it enhances your well-being and positively impacts those around you, creating a ripple effect of happiness in your relationships and communities.

THE LASTING JOY AFFIRMATIONS

69. I choose joy and happiness in every moment.

> Start your day by saying this with a smile, setting a positive tone for the hours ahead. This practice helps train your mind to seek and actively create joy throughout your day.

70. I am grateful for the abundance in my life.

> List three things you're grateful for each night, then affirm. This gratitude practice helps you focus on the posi-tive aspects of your life, fostering contentment.

71. I find joy in the journey, not just the destination.

> Say this while taking a walk, focusing on enjoying each step. This mindfulness exercise helps you appreciate the present moment and find joy in the process, not just outcomes.

72. I radiate positivity and attract joyful experiences.

> Visualize yourself as a beacon of light, attracting positive energy as you repeat this. This visualization reinforces your ability to influence your experiences through your attitude.

73. I embrace each day as a new opportunity for happiness.

> Say this as soon as you wake up, setting an intention for a joyful day. This morning ritual helps you approach each day with optimism and openness to joy.

74. I find beauty and wonder in the simple things of life.

> Practice saying this while observing nature or everyday objects with curiosity. This exercise enhances your appreciation for life's small joys, fostering a sense of wonder.

75. I cultivate inner peace that brings lasting joy.

> Repeat this during a meditation session, allowing the words to deepen your sense of peace. This practice connects inner calm with joy, reinforcing their relationship.

76. I choose to focus on the good in every situation.

> When faced with a challenge, say this while identifying one positive aspect. This reframing technique helps build resilience and maintain a positive outlook.

77. I am deserving of a life filled with laughter and joy.

> Say this while doing something that makes you laugh or smile. This practice reinforces the connection between joy and your sense of self-worth.

78. I embrace self-compassion as a source of lasting happiness.

> Place your hand on your heart and speak this affirmation with kindness to yourself. This gesture of self-love reinforces the importance of self-compassion in cultivating joy.

79. I find joy in connecting with others and building relationships.

> Before meeting friends or loved ones, repeat this to enhance your appreciation of connections. This practice helps you approach social interactions with positivity and openness.

80. I choose to let go of worry and embrace peace.

> Take a deep breath and exhale slowly while saying this, releasing tension. This physical act of releasing pairs with the affirmation to reinforce letting go of worry.

81. I am open to receiving joy and love in abundance.

> Stand with open arms as you say this, physically embodying receptiveness to joy. This posture helps you feel more open to positive experiences and emotions.

82. I find happiness in pursuing my passions and dreams.

> Say this before engaging in an activity you love, reinforcing the joy in your pursuits. This practice helps you connect your passions with joy, motivating you to pursue them.

83. I radiate joy and inspire happiness in others.

> Smile warmly while saying this, imagining your joy spreading to those around you. This visualization reinforces your ability to impact others positively through your own joy.

84. I choose to see opportunities for growth in every challenge.

> When facing a difficulty, repeat this while identifying a potential lesson or opportunity. This reframing technique helps you maintain a growth mindset and find positivity in challenges.

85. I am grateful for my body and all it does for me.

> Say this while doing gentle stretches, appreciating each part of your body. This practice fosters body positivity and gratitude for your physical health.

86. I find joy in expressing my creativity freely.

> Before starting a creative project, repeat this affirmation to connect with your creative joy. This practice helps you approach creative activities with enthusiasm and freedom.

87. I choose to surround myself with positive, uplifting people.

> Visualize yourself in the company of supportive friends while saying this affirmation. This visualization reinforces your commitment to cultivating positive relationships.

88. I embrace the present moment as a gift.

> Practice mindfulness while saying this, focusing on your senses and the present moment. This exercise helps you fully appreciate and find joy in the here and now.

89. I find lasting joy in personal growth and self-improvement.

> Say this before learning something new or working on a personal development goal. This affirmation connects joy with self-improvement, motivating your growth journey.

90. I radiate confidence, which brings me joy and fulfillment.

> Stand tall and smile while saying this, embodying confident joy. This physical embodiment reinforces the connection between confidence and joy.

91. I choose to release negative thoughts and embrace positivity.

> Visualize negative thoughts floating away like clouds as you repeat this affirmation. This visualization technique helps you let go of negativity and cultivate a positive mindset.

92. I find happiness in helping others and making a positive impact.

> Say this before engaging in acts of kindness or volunteer work. This practice reinforces the joy of altruism and motivates you to contribute positively to others' lives.

93. I embrace joy as my natural state of being.

> Place your hand on your heart and smile as you say this, connecting with your inner joy. This gesture helps you recognize and connect with your innate capacity for joy.

94. I choose to forgive, which frees me to experience more joy.

> Visualize releasing a burden while saying this, symbolizing the freedom of forgiveness. This practice reinforces the liberating effect of forgiveness on your joy.

95. I find pleasure and contentment in my daily routines.

> Say this while doing everyday tasks, finding joy in the mundane. This practice helps you appreciate and find happiness in your daily life.

96. I radiate love and compassion, which brings me lasting happiness.

> Visualize love flowing from your heart to others as you repeat this affirmation. This visualization reinforces the connection between compassion and personal happiness.

97. I choose to see the humor in life and laugh often.

> Say this before watching a comedy or engaging in a fun activity. This practice reminds you to seek out and appreciate humor in your life.

98. I find joy in caring for my mind, body, and spirit.

> Repeat this while engaging in self-care activities, reinforcing the joy of self-nurture. This affirmation validates the importance of holistic self-care in cultivating joy.

99. I embrace change as an opportunity for new joys and experiences.

> Say this when facing changes, reframing them as exciting new chapters. This perspective shift helps you approach change with optimism and openness.

100. I choose to create my own happiness, independent of circumstances.

> Repeat this when facing challenges, reminding yourself of your power to choose joy. This affirmation reinforces your agency in cultivating happiness regardless of external factors.

101. I am worthy of a life filled with lasting joy and fulfillment.

> End your day with this affirmation, intending continued joy. This practice reinforces your self-worth and sets a positive intention for ongoing happiness in your life.

Bonus #1

CULTIVATING PEACEFUL AND RESTFUL SLEEP

Cultivating peaceful and restful sleep is a fundamental pillar of health and well-being, yet quality sleep often eludes us in our fast-paced world. This bonus chapter focuses on harnessing the power of affirmations to create a mindset conducive to peaceful, restorative sleep.

These 33 sleep-focused affirmations are designed to help you:

- Release the day's stress and worries
- Calm your mind and relax your body
- Create positive associations with bedtime and sleep
- Boost your confidence in your ability to sleep well
- Cultivate gratitude for rest and renewal

By incorporating these affirmations into your bedtime

routine, you're setting the stage for more restful nights and energized days. Remember, good sleep is not just about quantity, but quality. These affirmations will help you approach sleep positively, potentially improving the dura-tion and depth of your rest.

Practice these affirmations as you prepare for bed, perhaps as part of a wind-down routine. Over time, your relationship with sleep may improve, leading to better overall health, increased daytime energy, and improved mental clarity.

SLEEP AFFIRMATIONS

1. I release the day's tensions and welcome peaceful sleep.

> Take a deep breath, exhaling slowly as you imagine the day's stress leaving your body.

2. My mind and body are ready for deep, restorative rest.

> Progressively relax each part of your body as you say this affirmation.

3. I trust in my ability to fall asleep easily and naturally.

> Place your hand over your heart, connecting with your innate ability to rest.

4. Each breath brings me closer to a state of calm relaxation.

> Synchronize this affirmation with slow, deep breaths.

5. I am safe, secure, and at peace in my sleeping environment.

> Look around your bedroom, appreciating the safety and comfort it provides.

6. My body knows how to sleep deeply and wake refreshed.

> Visualize yourself waking up feeling energized and refreshed.

7. I let go of all worry and embrace tranquility.

> Imagine worries floating away like clouds as you repeat this affirmation.

8. Sleep is a natural, healing process that I welcome.

> Smile gently as you say this, welcoming sleep as a friend.

9. I am grateful for the opportunity to rest and recharge.

> Picture yourself in your bedroom. Remind yourself how grateful you are to be sleeping in comfort and peace.

10. My mind becomes quiet as I prepare for restful sleep.

> Visualize a dimmer switch turning down the volume of your thoughts.

11. I deserve high-quality, rejuvenating sleep.

> Stand tall and state this confidently before getting into bed.

12. Falling asleep is easy and effortless for me.

> Visualize yourself falling asleep easily as you repeat this affirmation.

13. I release control and allow sleep to come naturally.

> Physically relax your body, letting go of any tension as you say this.

14. My bedroom is a sanctuary for peace and rest.

> Look around your room, appreciating its comfort as you say this.

15. I am in harmony with my natural sleep rhythms.

> Visualize your body's internal clock ticking in perfect rhythm.

16. Each night, my sleep quality improves.

> Imagine a graph showing your sleep quality improving over time.

17. I wake up feeling refreshed, energized, and ready for the day.

> Visualize yourself waking up with a smile, feeling great.

18. My mind and body know exactly how much sleep I need.

> Trust in your body's wisdom as you repeat this affirmation.

19. I let go of the day's events and embrace night's tranquility.

> Imagine closing a book titled "Today" as you say this.

20. Restful sleep comes to me easily and effortlessly.

> Visualize sleep as a gentle wave washing over you.

21. I am worthy of deep, replenishing sleep.

> Place your hand on your heart, acknowledging your worthiness of good rest.

22. My mind is calm, my body is relaxed, and I am ready for sleep.

> Do a quick body scan, relaxing each part as you say this.

23. I choose to let go of stress and welcome peaceful sleep.

> Imagine stress dissolving away as you repeat this affirmation.

24. Every cell in my body is preparing for rejuvenating rest.

> Visualize each cell in your body settling down for sleep.

25. I trust in the process of sleep to restore and heal me.

> Think of sleep as a healing light enveloping your body.

26. My dreams are positive and contribute to my well-being.

> Imagine pleasant dream scenarios as you say this affirmation.

27. I release negative thoughts and welcome calming ones.

> Visualize negative thoughts transforming into peaceful ones.

28. Sleep is a gift I give myself each night.

> Smile as you say this, appreciating the gift of rest.

29. I am becoming a better sleeper with each passing night.

> Visualize yourself mastering the art of sleep over time.

30. My evening routine prepares me perfectly for restful sleep.

> Review your bedtime routine in your mind, appreciating how it helps you.

31. I am at peace with myself and the world as I drift off to sleep.

> Take a deep breath, feeling a sense of peace wash over you.

32. My bed is comfortable and conducive to deep, restful sleep.

> Feel the comfort of your bed, appreciating its support.

33. I welcome the quiet and stillness of the night.

> Listen to the quiet around you, embracing the peace it brings.

EXTREME SELF CARE

INTRODUCTION TO AFFIRMATIONS FOR EXTREME SELF-CARE

This bonus chapter presents a powerful collection of 101 affirmations designed to boost your self-esteem, cultivate positivity, and promote extreme self-care. These carefully crafted statements cover various aspects of personal growth, from building confidence and resilience to fostering self-love and attracting abundance.

BENEFITS OF USING THESE AFFIRMATIONS

1. Improved self-image and confidence
2. Reduced stress and anxiety
3. Increased motivation and focus
4. Enhanced emotional well-being
5. Greater resilience in facing challenges

6. Improved relationships with yourself and others
7. Increased self-awareness and mindfulness
8. Alignment with your personal goals and values
9. Cultivation of a more positive mindset
10. Support for overall mental and emotional health

WHEN TO USE THESE AFFIRMATIONS

1. Morning routine: Start your day with positive self-talk
2. Before challenging situations: Boost confidence before important events
3. During moments of self-doubt: Combat negative thoughts
4. As part of a meditation or mindfulness practice
5. Before bed: End your day on a positive note
6. During self-care activities: Reinforce the importance of self-nurturing
7. When setting goals: Align your mindset with your aspirations
8. After facing setbacks: Build resilience and maintain a positive outlook

HOW BEST TO USE THESE AFFIRMATIONS

1. Choose affirmations that resonate with you personally.

2. Repeat each affirmation with conviction, preferably out loud.
3. Incorporate the suggested visualizations or physical actions to reinforce the message.
4. Practice consistently, ideally daily, for best results.
5. Believe in the words you're saying — let yourself feel their truth.
6. Adapt the affirmations to fit your personal situation if needed.
7. Use a mirror when possible to make eye contact with yourself.
8. Write down your favorite affirmations and place them where you'll see them often.
9. Record yourself saying the affirmations and listen to them throughout the day.
10. Combine affirmations with other self-care practices for a holistic approach to well-being.

Remember, the power of affirmations lies in their consistent practice and your belief in them. As you incorporate these positive statements in your regular routine, you will notice a shift in your mindset and an improvement in your overall sense of well-being.

AFFIRMATIONS

1. I am confident in my abilities and potential.

> Repeat this affirmation while standing tall with your shoulders back. Visualize yourself radiating confidence in various situations.

2. I embrace challenges as opportunities for growth.

> Say this while facing a mirror, making eye contact with yourself. Recall past challenges you've overcome to reinforce the belief.

3. My inner strength is limitless.

> Place your hand on your heart as you say this. Feel the warmth and power emanating from within.

4. I am worthy of success and happiness.

> Write this affirmation in your journal daily, allowing the words to manifest your worth physically.

5. I trust my intuition and make wise decisions.

> Close your eyes and take a deep breath before saying this. Imagine your intuition as a guiding light within you.

6. I radiate positivity and attract positive experiences.

> Say this while smiling, allowing your facial expression to reinforce the positive energy you're cultivating.

7. I am resilient and bounce back from setbacks more vital than ever.

> As you repeat this affirmation, visualize yourself as a flexible tree that bends but doesn't break in strong winds.

8. I am deserving of love, respect, and admiration.

> As you say these words, Place your hands on your heart and your stomach, connecting with your emotional centers.

9. My potential is infinite and I grow every day.

> Say this while stretching your arms wide, physically embodying the expansiveness of your potential.

10. I control my thoughts, feelings, and actions.

> Take three deep breaths before saying this, centering yourself and reinforcing your sense of control.

11. I embrace my uniqueness and celebrate my individuality.

> Say this while looking at your reflection, noting and appreciating your unique features.

12. I can achieve greatness in all areas of my life.

> Visualize yourself standing on a mountaintop, overlooking vast opportunities as you repeat this affirmation.

13. I attract abundance and prosperity effortlessly.

> As you say this, open your arms as if welcoming abundance into your life.

14. I am grateful for all the blessings in my life.

> Before bed, list three things you're grateful for, then say this affirmation to reinforce your appreciation.

15. I radiate confidence, self-respect, and inner harmony.

> Stand in a power pose (hands on hips, feet apart) while saying this affirmation.

16. I am worthy of living my dreams and pursuing my passions.

> Write down your most prominent dream, then say this affirmation while holding the paper to your heart.

17. I trust the journey of life and embrace its lessons.

> Say this while walking in nature, allowing the natural world to remind you of life's journey.

18. I am deserving of peace, joy, and fulfillment.

> Create a calm environment, light a candle, and repeat this affirmation meditatively.

19. I choose happiness and contentment in every moment.

> Start your day by saying this affirmation with a smile, setting a positive tone for the hours ahead.

20. I am confident in my ability to handle any situation.

> Recall a challenging situation you've overcome, then say this affirmation, drawing strength from your past success.

21. I embrace change and adapt quickly to new circumstances.

> Say this while consciously relaxing your body, releasing tension and resistance.

22. I am worthy of receiving good things in abundance.

> Open your hands palms up while saying this, as if physically receiving abundance.

23. I trust myself to make the best decisions for my life.

> Place your hand on your gut as you say this, connecting with your intuition.

24. I radiate love and compassion to myself and others.

> Say this while holding your hand over your heart, feeling warmth spread through your body.

25. I am empowered to create the life I desire.

> Visualize yourself as the architect of your life, drawing plans for your future as you repeat this affirmation.

26. I embrace my strengths and continue to develop them.

> List your top three strengths, then say this affirmation while focusing on each.

27. I deserve respect and healthy boundaries.

> Stand with your feet firmly planted and arms crossed as you say this, physically embodying your boundaries.

28. I attract positive and supportive people into my life.

> Visualize yourself surrounded by a golden light as you say this, attracting positive energy.

29. I am resilient and can overcome any obstacle.

> Say this while doing a physical activity that challenges you, reinforcing your resilience.

30. I trust in my ability to solve problems creatively.

> Before tackling a problem, gently repeat this affirmation while tapping your forehead.

31. I am worthy of living a life filled with joy and purpose.

> Write this affirmation on a sticky note and place it where you'll see it often throughout the day.

32. I embrace self-care and prioritize my well-being.

> Say this while engaging in a self-care activity, reinforcing the connection between the words and action.

33. I am confident in my ability to learn and grow.

> Before starting a new task or learning experience, repeat this affirmation to boost your confidence.

34. I radiate charisma and inspire others naturally.

> Practice saying this in front of a mirror, making eye contact and smiling confidently.

35. I trust the timing of my life and remain patient.

> Say this while taking slow, deep breaths, syncing the words with your breath to reinforce patience.

36. I am deserving of success and claim it confidently.

> Visualize yourself accepting an award or achieving a goal as you repeat this affirmation.

37. I embrace my power to create positive change.

> Say this before taking action on a goal or making a decision, reinforcing your ability to effect change.

38. I am worthy of love and give love freely.

> Place your hand on your heart and smile warmly as you say this, feeling the love within you.

39. I trust my journey and embrace each step with courage.

> Say this while stepping forward, physically embodying progress on your journey.

40. I radiate confidence and inspire confidence in others.

> Before entering a social situation, repeat this affirmation while standing tall and smiling.

41. I am resilient and grow stronger through challenges.

> Recall a problem you overcame, then affirm, drawing strength from your past resilience.

42. I embrace my authentic self and live true to my values.

> Write down your core values, then affirm them while looking at them.

43. I am deserving of abundance in all areas of my life.

> Say this while holding something representing abundance (e.g., a prosperous plant or a full wallet).

44. I trust in my ability to manifest my desires.

> Visualize your biggest goal as already achieved while repeating this affirmation.

45. I radiate positivity and attract positive outcomes.

> Start your day by saying this affirmation while looking out a window, imagining positivity spreading like sunlight.

46. I am confident in my ability to overcome any fear.

> Face something that scares you a little (e.g., looking over a balcony) while repeating this affirmation.

47. I embrace change as an opportunity for growth and renewal.

> Say this while rearranging a room or changing your appearance, physically embodying change.

48. I am worthy of achieving greatness in my chosen field.

> Before starting work or a project, repeat this affirmation to set a tone of excellence.

49. I trust my intuition to guide me towards my highest good.

> As you say this, Place your hand on your stomach (your "gut"), connecting with your intuitive center.

50. I radiate self-love and treat myself with kindness.

> Look in the mirror and say this affirmation while giving yourself a warm, approving smile.

51. I am empowered to set and achieve ambitious goals.

> Write down a big goal, then say this affirmation while holding the paper to your forehead, as if imprinting it on your mind.

52. I embrace my unique gifts and share them confidently with the world.

> Say this before engaging in an activity that showcases your talents or skills.

53. I deserve to live a life that excites and fulfills me.

> Create a vision board of your ideal life, then affirm it while looking at it.

54. I trust in my ability to handle whatever comes my way.

> Say this while standing in a "superhero pose" (hands on hips, feet apart, chin up), embodying strength and readiness.

55. I radiate inner peace and maintain calm in all situations.

> Practice saying this during a meditation session, allowing the words to deepen your sense of peace.

56. I am confident in expressing my thoughts and ideas.

> Before a meeting or conversation, repeat this affirmation while taking deep, grounding breaths.

57. I embrace each day as a new opportunity for joy and growth.

> Say this as soon as you wake up, setting a positive tone for the day ahead.

58. I am worthy of respect and command it through my actions.

> Stand tall with your shoulders back as you say this, physically embodying self-respect.

59. I trust my ability to create positive change in my life.

> Say this before deciding on or taking action towards a goal, reinforcing your power to effect change.

60. I radiate enthusiasm and inspire others with my energy.

> Jump or dance in place while saying this affirmation, physically expressing your enthusiasm.

61. I am resilient and bounce back stronger from every setback.

> Visualize yourself as a rubber band, stretching and snapping back into shape as you repeat this affirmation.

62. I embrace my power to choose my reactions and attitudes.

> Take a deep breath and pause before responding to a situation, saying this affirmation to remind yourself of your power of choice.

63. I deserve to celebrate my accomplishments, big and small.

> At the end of each day, list three accomplishments and say this affirmation while reviewing them.

64. I trust in my ability to build meaningful and lasting relationships.

> Repeat this affirmation to boost your interpersonal confidence before meeting someone new or deepening an existing relationship.

65. I radiate gratitude and find joy in everyday moments.

> Start a gratitude journal and say this affirmation each time you write an entry, reinforcing your appreciation for life.

66. I am confident in my ability to learn from every experience.

> After facing a challenge or making a mistake, say this affirmation while reflecting on the lessons learned.

67. I embrace my journey of personal growth with enthusiasm.

> Create a personal growth plan and say this affirmation each time you work on it, reinforcing your commitment to self-improvement.

68. I am worthy of experiencing abundant love and affection.

> Place your hands over your heart as you say this, allowing yourself to feel worthy of love.

69. I trust in my ability to make wise financial decisions.

> This affirmation reinforces your financial wisdom before making a budget or financial plan.

70. I radiate health and vitality from every cell of my body.

> Say this while doing light exercise or stretching, connecting the affirmation with physical wellness.

71. I am empowered to create healthy habits and stick to them.

> Write down a healthy habit you want to cultivate, then say this affirmation while looking at it.

72. I embrace my creativity and express it freely.

> Before starting a creative project, repeat this affirmation while holding a symbol of creativity (e.g., a paintbrush or notebook).

73. I am deserving of taking time for self-care and relaxation.

> Say this while engaging in a relaxing activity, reinforcing the importance of self-care.

74. I trust in my ability to communicate effectively and assertively.

> Practice saying this before a meaningful conversation, boosting your confidence.

75. I radiate confidence in my unique style and self-expression.

> Say this while getting dressed or looking in the mirror, appreciating your unique style.

76. I am resilient in the face of criticism and use it for growth.

> After receiving feedback, repeat this affirmation while writing down how to use the input constructively.

77. I embrace my ability to inspire and motivate others.

> Before giving advice or mentoring someone, say this affirmation to tap into your inspirational qualities.

78. I am worthy of pursuing and achieving my dreams.

> Create a dream board and say this affirmation while visualizing each dream becoming reality.

79. I trust in my ability to maintain a positive mindset.

> Start your day by saying this affirmation while smiling, setting the tone for positive thinking.

80. I radiate compassion and understanding toward myself.

> Say this while placing one hand on your heart and extending the other outward, symbolizing compassion for yourself.

81. I am confident in adapting to new technologies and ideas.

> Before learning something new, repeat this affirmation to boost your adaptability and openness.

82. I embrace opportunities to step out of my comfort zone.

> Say this before doing something that challenges you, reinforcing your courage to grow.

83. I am deserving of work that fulfills and excites me.

> Write down your ideal job or project, then say this affirmation while visualizing yourself in that role.

84. I trust my ability to build and maintain a healthy body and mind.

> Say this while doing a body scan meditation, connecting with each part of your body and mind.

85. I radiate leadership qualities and inspire others to excel.

> Before taking on a leadership role or task, repeat this affirmation while standing tall and confident.

86. I am empowered to create healthy boundaries in all my relationships.

> Practice saying this before entering a social situation, reminding yourself of your right to set boundaries.

87. I embrace my unique perspective and value my opinions.

> Before sharing your thoughts in a meeting or conversation, say this affirmation to boost your confidence in your viewpoint.

88. I am worthy of surrounding myself with supportive and positive people.

> Visualize yourself in the company of supportive friends while saying this affirmation, attracting positive relationships.

89. I trust in my ability to solve any problem creatively.

> Before brainstorming or problem-solving, repeat this affirmation to tap into your creative potential.

90. I radiate inner strength and overcome obstacles with ease.

> Say this while flexing your muscles, physically embodying your inner strength.

91. I am confident in my ability to manage my time effectively.

> Before planning your day or week, repeat this affirmation to reinforce your time management skills.

92. I embrace the present moment and find joy in the now.

> Practice mindfulness while saying this affirmation, focusing on your senses and the present moment.

93. I deserve a life filled with adventure and new experiences.

> Say this before trying something new or planning a trip, opening yourself to adventure.

94. I trust in my ability to forgive and let go of past hurts.

> Visualize releasing a balloon while saying this affirmation, symbolizing letting go of past pain.

95. I radiate authenticity and attract genuine connections.

> Before meeting new people, say this affirmation to remind yourself of the value of authenticity.

96. I am resilient in the face of change and uncertainty.

> During times of change, repeat this affirmation while taking deep, calming breaths.

97. I embrace my power to impact the world positively.

> Before engaging in a volunteer activity or helping someone, say this affirmation to connect with your ability to make a difference.

98. I am worthy of living a life aligned with my deepest values.

> Write down your core values and say this affirmation while reading them, reinforcing your commitment to living authentically.

99. I trust in the unfolding of my life's purpose.

> Say this while meditating or in a quiet moment, allowing yourself to feel connected to your life's journey.

100. I radiate unconditional self-love and acceptance.

> Look in the mirror and say this affirmation while touching your heart, fully accepting yourself.

101. I am the architect of my destiny, creating a life of joy and fulfillment.

> Say this while visualizing yourself building your ideal life, brick by brick, empowering yourself as the creator of your destiny.

About the Author

Melissa G. Wilson's remarkable book writing, coaching, and publishing career is a testament to her expertise, innovation, and unwavering commitment to helping others succeed. With a portfolio of ten books published by six traditional publishers, including five bestsellers, Wilson has established herself as a prominent figure in the literary world.

Her seventh book, "Networlding," achieved extraordinary success, maintaining the #10 position on Amazon across all categories for a year. Another of her works climbed to the prestigious Wall Street Journal bestseller list, further solidifying her reputation as a prolific and influential author.

Wilson's expertise has garnered significant media attention, with one of her books featured on Oprah's influential platform. She has also appeared on major television programs, including the Today Show and other national broadcasts, expanding her reach and impact as a thought leader.

In 2010, Wilson founded Networlding Publishing, a venture that expertly combines her deep networking knowledge with her extensive book writing, publishing, and coaching background. This innovative approach has empowered authors to build vibrant networks and enhance their careers and businesses through thought-leadership books.

Her dedication to client success is unwavering, as evidenced by the impressive roster of over 174 thought leaders she has guided through the writing, publishing, and launching process. Her clients include high-profile individuals such as the head of diversity for Hewitt, the Chief Digital Officer of Cisco, a seven-time Inc. 500 entrepreneur, and Tom Peters, a bestselling author with 4.5 million books sold.

Wilson's innovative spirit is a driving force that keeps her at the forefront of the publishing industry. She was part of Seth Godin's Domino Project Street Team, co-created the "Seven Problems of Marketing" series for the American Marketing Association, and contributed to launching a new line of books for the American Bar Association. These accomplishments showcase her ability to tackle industry challenges and drive positive change, inspiring others to do the same.

What sets apart Wilson's latest book has its foundation in her journey of using affirmations to succeed as a book creation expert and coach. Drawing from years of experience, she demonstrates the transformative power of positive self-talk and mindset in realizing one's goals. This book is a guide and a reflection of Wilson's own path to success, offering readers authentic insights and proven strategies.

Wilson's unwavering commitment to wellness, better living, and particularly to supporting women in their life journeys, makes her an author and thought leader worth following. Her holistic approach to success, which combines professional expertise with personal growth techniques, resonates with readers seeking both career advancement and personal fulfillment. By sharing her experiences with affirmations and their impact on her success, Wilson provides a unique and valuable perspective that can inspire and guide others on their own paths to achievement.

As an advocate for women's empowerment and overall well-being, Wilson's work extends beyond the realm of publishing and networking. She consistently uses her platform to promote positive lifestyle changes, encouraging her readers and clients to prioritize their mental and emotional health alongside their professional goals.

This comprehensive approach to success and personal development distinguishes Melissa in the crowded field of self-help and business literature, making her an influential voice for those seeking to improve their careers and lives holistically. Her commitment to wellness and women's empowerment provides her readers and clients with a supportive and encouraging environment.

Before You Go

"Your book review can be a beacon for curious minds. Keep it straightforward and genuine. Your unique perspective will greatly help others."

ANONYMOUS

It has been an honor and a pleasure sharing my experiences as a busy executive and as someone who was, once upon a time, a working mother and a new employee. We all start at the beginning.

The world needs you and your significant impact. My goal with this book was to help you find the motivation and opportunities to win in big ways—exponential wins that extend to your customers, peers, company and shareholders, vendors, and ultimately, our families and communities. The opportunities are endless, and they all start with you.

BEFORE YOU GO

Before you go, I have a simple request. Authors rely heavily on reviews for their success, so I would greatly appreciate it if you would please take a few minutes to leave an honest review.

Don't hesitate to contact me with any questions you might have by emailing me at **melissa@networlding.com**.

I'm also available for coaching at a lower price than most coaches charge. Why? As best-selling author Mark Schaefer stated about me when I took his branding class:

"Melissa is the most caring book coach in the world."

Navigate to **https://networlding.com/one-one-coaching/** for more information.

Here's to your success.
Melissa

www.ingramcontent.com/pod-product-compliance
Lightning Source LLC
Chambersburg PA
CBHW061338040426
42444CB00011B/2974